My Happiness High

(A guide to stay happy-no matter what!)

ISBN: 9798574355817
Imprint: Independently published

Cover design by: Art Painter
Library of Congress Control Number: 2018675309
Printed in India

CONTENTS

Acknowledgement

This is my third book and I am very thankful for all the supportive people around me who considered this aspect of my personality as a valuable one and gave it the required spark.

I would start with thanking my ever-supportive husband, who believes in all my whims and fancies and has been an immense support and a pillar of strength whenever I needed him. He is protective and sensitive and yet has the knack to know when to let me have my way. I am blessed to have him in my life. He is the one who has given me the cognizance that I have the ability to fly. He is my wings.

My mentor, my Guru, Ms. Anuradha Gupta who believed in me and always guided me towards improving my present circumstances, be it in my personal life or my professional one. I can't thank God enough for sending her angelic presence in my life!

Ms. Uttara Singh, the Director of Shriram Millennium Schools, Ms. Sonali Gupta, the Principal of my school and Ms. Annapurna Das, the Vice Principal of my school have always supported me in reinventing myself and becoming a better version of myself. I can't thank them enough for their constant support.

With all your blessings I wish that my efforts are fruitful and my dreams are realized.

Happy reading!

Love: Mahi

Happiness- What is it?

Happiness means the state of being positive and interested in the world around you. When one feels that the present situation or circumstance is the most desirable and should continue the way it is.

According to Wikipedia Berkley *'The term happiness is used in the context of mental or emotional states, including positive or pleasant emotions ranging from contentment to intense joy. It is also used in the context of life satisfaction, subjective well-being, eudaimonia, flourishing and well-being.'*

"Life is like a sandwich!
Birth as one slice,
and death as the other.
What you put in-between
the slices is up to you.
Is your sandwich tasty or sour?

Allan Rufus, in the above lines tries to tell us that it is up to us how we spend our lives. Whether we are happy or sad, ecstatic or dismal, optimistic or pessimistic, excited or apprehensive is all in our own hands.

Yesterday I received the author copies of my recent book and I was ecstatic to hold it in my hands for the first time.

My brother's wife was blessed with a baby girl and on hearing the news my brother jumped with joy.

My mother had tears of happiness in her eyes on receiving the news of her soldier son coming back home safely after being away for two years at war.

She saw her crush taking the seat next to her in the classroom and a smile lit her face.

She lifted the cup for the National Championship with pride.

She saw her student speaking confidently on stage and wiped a tear of joy remembering the time when he used to suffer from stage fright.

She looked at the snow-capped mountain peaks with exhilaration while getting ready for the climb.

She sipped her tea and turned the page of the book smiling to herself.

He rested his head on the wall behind him listening to the soulful music reverberating in the chords of his heart.

The sound of lake water lapping against the shores.

The smell of fresh grass.

The sound of church bells.

The smell of fresh bread.

The smell of rain after the hot and dusty weather.

The cry of a new born child.

The chirping of birds early in the morning.

The smell of fresh mangoes straight from the orchard.

The smell of coffee.

The sound of hymns.

Raindrops falling on your eyelashes and lips.

Walking silently hand in hand with your beloved.

The list can go on and on but just by reading some of these beautiful experiences we feel elated and positive. This is the power of reiteration. Happiness generates more happiness.

'Happiness is not something ready-made, it comes from your own actions'- well I didn't say that the

14th Dalai Lama said it and it holds a lot of water.

Happiness is within you and your circumstances and the people around you cannot make you happy unless you are happy from within. I vouch for this but to tell you the truth it isn't as easy as it sounds. Making yourself happy from within doesn't come without effort just like our very own Dalai Lama suggested. So, what is it that we need to do to continue being in a state of happiness and not losing sight of it?

It is a step by step process that helps you master your brain to be in a happy state and not let adversities affect you or keep you low for a long time. One needs to bounce back and carry on because adversities will definitely come and we just need the tools to manoeuvre our way around these stumbling blocks.

In the following chapters we are going to go step by step towards our goal of being ever blissful or rather being on a 'happiness high' and not losing sight of our positivity in any circumstances.

Let me add here that when I say that we need to be happy or be in a state of 'happiness high' I don't mean that there won't be any setbacks or if there are negative moments or we go through down-time in life we are losers or we have lost our battle. Our aim is to tide over such situations and move on into the direction of being blissful and optimistic again. The achievement of 'happiness high' is our goal and it can bc achicvcd by anyone. That's the good news!

Seven Habits of Happiness High

Habit one- Solitude

There's a huge difference between being alone and being lonely. When you learn to be happy in your own company then you can never be lonely. Each person is advised to find out some 'alone time' every day to be able to catch up with the emotions building up and the thoughts and ideas crowding your mind. Being alone gives you time to declutter your system and get more organized. Once you are organized and have a hold of the situation around you, nobody can stop you from acquiring self-affirmations. Like Mary Sarton says:

"I simply adore being alone – I find it a consuming thirst – and when that thirst is slaked, then I am happy."

Once you have realised the importance of being in your own company it will become easier for you to accept yourself the way you are and be happy and comfortable in your own skin. One who is at peace with himself/herself has nothing to stop him/her from being happy. You need to be able to bear your own company how else can you expect the others to bear with you?
Loneliness is to be avoided; solitude is to be sought."– Tom Hanks
When Tom Hanks said the above lines, he meant that solitude is not

the only ingredient for happiness because it can quickly turn to loneliness. What is important is that you are able to seek solitude, it isn't thrust upon you. Solitude is wilful whereas loneliness is forced. Your mind and your circumstances are in conflict when you are lonely. To be in conflict is not good for your happiness. To be able to enjoy your solitude you need to be craving for it, you need to be looking forward to it and you need to have enough practice in that art.

How can you practice this art? Well more on it later in the detailed chapter. For now, just remember the words of Paulo Coelho:

Solitude is not the absence of company, but the moment when our soul is free to speak to us and help us decide what to do with our life."

Habit two- Honesty

'If you were completely honest to yourself about yourself, other people and the world, you would never get disappointed. You would liberate yourself from all the illusions and falsehoods. This would give you great power.' -The Ancient Sage

We all have heard that 'honesty is the best policy' and believe me it is the most underrated statement ever. Being honest in all circumstances is possible and is a very important step towards true happiness. A person who is honest is never under the pressure of remembering what he said and how much has to be divulged. S/he can freely speak up whatever S/he wants to say without worrying about being judged.

Some people might think that it is not possible to be completely honest all the time and some might think that if we always speak the truth, we might end up in unfavourable situations which could be detrimental for us. I want to say a big 'NO' to that. I will explain how you can be honest always and still be happy and 'safe'. In the meantime, chew on this:

Honesty is a very expensive gift. Don't expect it from cheap people. Warren Buffett

Habit three- Self love

"Remember, you have been criticizing yourself for years, and it hasn't worked. Try approving of yourself and see what happens."- Louise L. Hay

The wise words of Louise L Hay hold a lot of sense and I can vouch for it myself. I had been and I tend to be still (old habits die late!) very critical of myself which leads to a lot of unhappiness because if you are picky you will definitely get enough to pick at.

You have to realise that we are all humans and we tend to have drawbacks, shortcomings, weaknesses, disgusting pasts, unfavourable features and glaring mistakes. What we need is acceptance of all of your negative aspects and resolve to overcome it or ignore it if it is impossible to resolve. In other words, make peace with it.

What you think of yourself and how you present yourself to the others plays a large role in how they will perceive you. When I say that, it doesn't mean to start praising yourself and projecting yourself falsely because when following the third habit we cannot forget the second habit. We have to be honest and we need not lie either to others or to ourselves to accept us the way we are. How to make that a reality is something we will learn in detail in the third habit.

"A healthy self-love means we have no compulsion to justify to ourselves or others why we take vacations, why we sleep late, why we buy new shoes, why we spoil ourselves from time to time. We feel comfortable doing things which add quality and beauty to life." - Andrew Matthews

Habit four- Attitude

When you face a choice between being polite and being honest, err on the side of the truth. It's better to be disliked but respected than to be liked but disrespected. In the long run, the people we trust the most are those who have the courage to be sincere. - Adam Grant

We have often heard that attitude is everything. If we learn to do with a smile what we have to do anyway, we can do it with a more positive attitude. "I do not believe in taking the right decision, I take a decision and make it right."- Muhammad Ali Jinnah

So many times, when we go through life we come across situations where we feel dejected, humiliated, dissatisfied, judged, undermined and unhappy. Well, if I say that how we feel depends on our attitude towards that situation you will think I am joking. I am definitely not joking. I mean it.

Having a positive attitude doesn't come easily. It's a fine balance between reality and hallucination. We will learn the tricks and a step by step method of mastering the art in the detailed chapter based on the habit. For now, just remember what Walt Whitman said, 'Keep your face always towards the sunshine - and shadows will fall behind you.'

Habit five- Dream and aspire!

Well, we have often heard: what is life without a dream?

Consult not your fears but your hopes and your dreams. Think not about your frustrations, but about your unfulfilled potential. Concern yourself not with what you tried and failed in, but with what it is still possible for you to do. - Pope John XXIII

An aimless mind and a free person have a lot of time to cultivate negativity. When you are occupied you have no time to regret or worry about what you don't have because there is enough to focus on what you can have. Just being occupied is not enough, you need to feel motivated to carry out the tasks you have at hand. Motivation comes from the fact that there's a personal achievement in the task that you are doing. Now some people will find it difficult to associate themselves with the drab and boring jobs they are expected to accomplish. The clue lies in looking for the personal motivation in anything that you are expected to complete. We'll talk about how to personally associate yourself with anything that you are expected to do in the fifth habit chapter. Dreams and dedication are a powerful combination and once we understand that 'mantra' we can accomplish anything.

'The future belongs to those who believe in the beauty of their dreams' said Eleanor Roosevelt.

Once you begin to believe that you are close to your dream and you have the aspiration to fulfil it you have no room left for negativity. At times it does become difficult to keep yourself motivated thus and the only advice at such moments is that one must hold onto the dream and wait for the negativity to pass over and then continue with the same zeal. It is much easier to do that than it sounds and before we delve into it stick to the thought;

'Hold fast to dreams, for if dreams die, life is a broken-winged bird that cannot fly.' -Langston Hughes

Habit six- Conversation

So many people must have said to us time and again that every problem can be resolved with a conversation. Communication is a tricky terrain because it is a two-way activity. You cannot expect the other person to be able to grasp everything the way you have expressed it as there are many barriers to communication like attitude, temperament, circumstances, education, upbringing and so on and so forth. So even if this sounds the easiest it is the trickiest of all the tools we have discussed. Let us begin with why communication is important.

"The single biggest problem in communication is the illusion that it has taken place." - George Bernard Shaw

Well, unless the source of your problem or unhappiness, which may sometimes be another person or situation, knows the effect it is creating, it cannot withdraw the effect. One other loophole and a greater danger could be to make yourself vulnerable in front of the source of your problem and communicating and explaining exactly what and how to hurt you further. Well, do not worry because this tool becomes as powerful and effective as the others if you combine it with the other tools we have discussed. We'll get to know how.

"To effectively communicate, we must realize that we are all different in the way we perceive the world and use this understanding as a guide to our communication with others." - Anthony Robbins

Habit seven- Gratitude

Gratitude is a powerful catalyst for happiness. It's the spark that lights a fire of joy in your soul." – Amy Collette

Gratitude is something that you cannot fake. The moment you don't feel it; it becomes flattery. So, gratitude has a lot to do with the habit of honesty and the habit of solitude. How are they related? Well, you need to speak, feel or express gratitude genuinely or else it loses its effect and to be able to feel it in its true sense you need to connect with yourself which comes naturally through the habit of solitude. Why is it so important to feel or express gratitude? It keeps you grounded and it keeps you positive. Once you feel the positive vibes flow through your persona you feel happy which is our ultimate goal.

"Happiness cannot be travelled to, owned, earned, worn or consumed. Happiness is the spiritual experience of living every minute with love, grace, and gratitude." - said Denis Waitley, and we couldn't agree more.

It isn't something that you can achieve by force or compulsion it has to come naturally from within. We will understand how to imbibe gratitude in ourselves naturally.

Extra Dose- Stay away from denial.

Denial is a coping mechanism that gives you time to adjust to distressing situations — but staying in denial can interfere with treatment or your ability to tackle challenges. If you're in denial, you're trying to protect yourself by refusing to accept the truth about something that's happening in your life. (Mayo Clinic)

Never feel scared of facing the music. Most people tend to extend their period of sadness and negativity by denying the acceptance and looking for redressal. They tend to avoid and ignore the issue till it becomes a deep wound which takes even more time to heal. Remember what the age-old granny says, 'A stich in time saves nine!'

Habit 1- Solitude

Follow Mahi. Author for more quotes on yourquote.in

Habit 1- Solitude

For oft, when on my couch I lie
In vacant or in pensive mood,
They flash upon that inward eye
Which is the bliss of solitude;
And then my heart with pleasure fills,
And dances with the daffodils.

William Wordsworth

The famous poem 'Daffodils' was written by William Wordsworth to describe how the therapeutic power of Nature helps him ride over the dismal circumstances around him and moves him towards light and positivity. He talks about lying on his couch in a vacant and pensive mood and dwell in solitude thinking about the beautiful sight of the innumerable daffodils he had seen in the valley on a similar dismal day which turned out to be a real mood lifter for him. He gives us a lesson that being in your own company gives you time to look within.

I have met people who are scared or uncomfortable in their own company because they have still not found a connection with their soul. It is natural for us to be a bit disconnected in the times that we are living in. There is so much happening around us, there's chaos all around and life is so fast paced that we hardly get time to connect with ourselves. Our confidence keeps dwindling, keeps alleviating with the increasing gap between the person we are to the world and the person we are within.

Let me tell you a small incident. Once when I was a teacher in a school in another country, I was observed by the Vice principal for my teaching skills and after the session she came up to me and gave me some negative feedback about my attitude. It was a demonstration class and I had been out of touch for a long time but I strongly felt that as a teacher, attitude is something that is inherent and cannot be taught. I felt very demotivated and unhappy with the feedback. I couldn't think of trying anywhere else and I just returned home. At home, there were my husband and his sister and we all spent some time talking. They asked me about the demo class and I didn't really know what to say. I told them that it was bad and I didn't expect to be called. This confession made me lighter and I moved out from the humdrum and escaped to my room on the pretext of needing some space.

I went to my room and played some soft music and lay down on my bed. I was relaxed because I had no expectations and I didn't even want to think about it. I closed my eyes and felt the music reverberate through my body. It was such a sweet lull that I didn't realise when I was fast asleep. I had not slept so soundly in the last few months because I had been preparing for my demonstration classes and other interviews. Well, when I got up, I was so relaxed and very positive after a very long time. I looked at myself in the mirror and said to myself, "This isn't the last school in this city. You aren't a bad teacher and you know it! So, let's just rejoice because it is their loss and not yours."

On other such occasions I just retreat into my 'Me-space' and pamper myself with some good music and beauty sleep and once the mood passes, I feel as fresh as ever. Giving yourself the much needed me-time is essential as connecting to your soul is a big remedy to cure any negativity. Our soul is a part of the ultimate source of energy whom we all pray to and at times take for granted but it is nonetheless the guiding light which tells us when we go wrong and how to bounce back from any negative situation.

What I would want to reiterate here though, is that unless you understand the difference between loneliness and solitude, this step would not be meaningful and will not bear any fruits.

"Solitude isn't loneliness. Solitude is when the entire serene universe seems to surround and hold you quietly."– Victoria Erickson

Solitude is a sought-after state and loneliness is a forced one.

"It's okay if you discover you love being alone. Who says you should not?"– Maxime Lagacé

Let me demonstrate the difference between loneliness and solitude through an incident. One of my colleagues, Reshmi, lost her father. She was an only child of her father and she had lost her mother when she was just a few months old. When she lost her father, she sent a message to her close friend, Namita, to convey the message to school. Namita knew that Reshmi was a recluse and didn't like too many people around her so she decided to go to her after a day or two when she would be more comfortable to handle the situation. She didn't forward the message to anyone in the office too to maintain her privacy.

After two days when she went to the colleague's house, she found her in a bad shape. She was told by the relatives and neighbours that after her father's death she was so fraught with depression that she had to be taken to a psychiatrist. She realised after speaking to the doctor that Reshmi was a recluse by nature so she didn't have many friends and since she had lost her mother early in life and now her father too, there weren't many relatives either who had kept in touch with them. At that juncture of life, she needed someone to open up to and at that moment there was no one with her. Her only friend who had received her message had not shown up and she was feeling so lonely that she couldn't control her mental state from slipping into depression. So basically, Namita was trying to give her space but what she didn't realise was that Reshmi needed her company. She didn't ask for that 'space' so she felt lonely and this wasn't her moment of solitude.

What we must understand when we come face to face with such situations is, that we must always be available for our friends and be very cautious even when they ask to be left alone. Understanding genuinely when we should leave them alone and when we should stick around is very important. Loneliness is a killer, and solitude is a saviour. So be very careful. If on being alone you can't help but think negatively then it isn't the rule to stick to. Go out and meet people and discuss your problems, rather than trying to resolve it through solitude.

So, the golden rule of solitude is to take a deep breath, talk to your inner self and check whether it is working. If it is taking you deeper into an abyss of negativity, if it's not releasing any positive signs; abandon it and try another way.

Once you have learnt to differentiate between solitude and loneliness you must understand how to use your 'me-time.'

How to maximise the benefits of this solitude? The three most important things that cause happiness to flow out into your life and create a blissful mood are:

1. Yoga/Dance
2. Music-Play or Listen
3. Sleep/Read/Draw/Write

Mostly when we are in a negative mood, we are either overwhelmed, or stressed or overworked. To release this negative knot, we need to open our hearts. The tried and tested effects of these three sets of activities can be verified by looking up the benefits of these on 'google' or any other search engine of your choice. The results will be the same.

Some people who aren't trained in Yoga or dance can just stretch and perform deep breathing exercises which will have a similar calming effect on them. As far as dancing is concerned when you are in solitude there's no one to judge you, so just play the music of your choice and let your hair loose. Just dance to your heart's content and release all the negativity and feel the flow of positive energy that revitalises you and soothes your mind.

Listening to music of your choice also has a similar effect. Some prefer rock, while some prefer soft, soothing music. Whatever your choice is, just indulge yourself. Some people are lucky to have learnt the art of playing different kinds of musical instruments like guitar, drums, saxophone, piano, flute or any other. Whether you play your own music or listen to your favourite music it is bound to have a positive effect on you. So, play on- it is famously known as the 'food of love' by the great playwright 'William Shakespeare' and it definitely is!

The woods are lovely dark and deep,

But I have promises to keep,

And miles to go before I sleep,

And miles to go before I sleep.

(Stopping by woods on a snowy evening- by Robert Frost)

Sleep is very important for a healthy mind and body and we all know about the effects of sleep deprivation. A lot of our negativity is also due to sleep deprivation. So many times, we don't even realise why we are feeling cranky, hungry and brain fogged. Yes, the answer is sleep deprivation. Catching up on your sleep can not just give you some escape from your bad mood, it can also help you keep yourself healthier and more focussed.

When we sleep well, we avoid overeating or kummerspeck, we avoid unnecessary stress and wastage of time and energy on negativity. This helps us to keep away from getting overweight, having issues like diabetes, thyroid malfunction, confusion or fogginess, low sex drive, weakened immunity, high blood pressure, memory related issues and mood swings. One beautiful activity which requires nothing but your ability to relax can save you from so many problems. So, grab a pillow and see your sad moments melt away into a deep relaxing sleep. Once you will wake up from your sleep you will find a glow on your face that you have been missing from days. Throw that expensive cream out of the window for the best and most inexpensive solution for your beauty is your beauty sleep.

Well, sometimes when the stress levels are too high you can't just lie down and fall off to sleep. What should you do then? Choose your favourite mode of expression. Do you love to draw, or write or read books? Pick it up and do it with a vengeance. Yes, you heard it right. Keep colour pencils and crayons handy and just scribble or draw whatever you feel like. The colours the action of drawing lines on paper helps you release the toxins you are holding inside of you. Maybe initially the art work you make isn't worth looking at but after a while you will see that once you've scribbled enough and done a lot of art work you start getting creative ideas and who knows maybe you will end up making one of your masterpieces! Kudos!

Some people are great at expressing their emotions through writing. Keep a journal and I would suggest just keep loose sheets in a file or use a spiral bound notebook where you can easily pull out the sheets and destroy them. Once you have vented out your anger and your sorrow on a piece of paper you can pull it out of your journal and just cut it up into pieces or tear it up. It is a liberating feeling to do that. Try it. At times when you have really been overwhelmed and you are expressing yourself you can end up making a beautiful piece of poetry or a really poignant description which can be a highly valuable piece of literature. Who knows you might just end up writing an award-winning poem or a heart touching song! Sell it and earn your royalty for life.

Reading self-help books can be highly helpful though most of them will just reiterate what you already know but it is important to be reminded of certain things that we tend to forget or take for granted. It helps. Yes, it does. Reading a mystery story or an adventure can shift your focus and take you to a land where your own problem will become inconsequential. You will laugh it off as you will realise what kind of complications can occur if one gets a little risk-loving. Reading a fiction book or a social drama will amuse you. You may empathise with the characters or you may find them ridiculous or funny but it will definitely shift your focus and take you into a different world and show you a different paradigm. So, choose your distraction but do give yourself your much deserved 'space' and enjoy your solitude.

"A man can be himself so long as he is alone. If he does not love solitude, he will not love freedom; for it is only when he is alone that he is really free."– Arthur Schopenhauer

Habit 2- Honesty

Follow Mahi. Author for more quotes on yourquote.in

Habit 2- Honesty

It is a very old and trusted belief that if you tell the truth you don't need to remember what you have told anyone. Speaking the truth and being honest always is definitely possible and who can teach this to us better than Lord Buddha himself. There are various stories where Buddha was challenged to speak the truth even though it could lead him to a precarious situation. He not only told the truth but also saved himself from the precarious situation.

Honesty means being true to oneself and to one's every moment of life. It means no fabrication, no pretence, no foolishness. It means to be simple. To be truly mindful of everything and giving it its due respect.

No matter how plain a woman may be, if truth and honesty are written across her face, she will be beautiful.
- Eleanor Roosevelt

While the above quote is said for a woman, we must honestly accept that it applies to everyone regardless of the gender. The tricky part though is the fact that how can we always be honest? Sometimes it becomes imperative to lie or people will take your simplicity and straightforwardness for granted. NO. That is absolutely wrong. Anyone who believes that, is either unaware of how to use the power of honesty effectively or has got into the web of making excuses.

Well according to Buddhism, honesty is one of the paths described in the eight-fold path of Buddhism.

Real honesty means to accept things the way they are. Not to try to change them. Honesty means to believe in what we see and accept it as reality. But we humans are in constant denial of the reality around us. We don't accept what is, and always try to see it through a lens of what should be. This drains us of our energy and fills us up with anxiety. When we accept things the way they are we are being honest to it and to ourselves.

Now for example, suppose we are jealous of someone because they have achieved something that we have not, and if we deny the emotion and continue to simmer and feel the need to deny the feeling and try to cover it with other emotions, we continue to be dishonest. We spend a lot of energy in fighting that emotion and trying to deviate our focus from it but once we accept it and give it its due respect, we address it head on. We need to be honest with whatever emotion or situation we are in. Once we have done that it will stop bothering us. That's not just a religious teaching, it is scientifically proven. Thus, honesty remains the best policy for evermore.

Let us move on to more complex situations where we need to be honest.

If it is not right do not do it; if it is not true do not say it.-Marcus Aurelius

Well, the more complex a situation is, the simpler the rule is. If it's not right, don't do it; as simple as that.

For example, if your child has been told from the beginning the adverse effects of smoking, alcoholism, drug abuse, unprotected sex or unnecessary violence then when s/he gets into a situation like this, s/he knows that it is not right. There is no dilemma. So many times, we ourselves do not know how to empower our children and how to make them aware of the right and wrong things and when they get into a soup, we blame them. That approach is dishonest. Accept that you did not do your duty right. You did not empower them with the correct information and values. Accept it and you will be at peace because then you won't look for a person to blame. You will have respected the feeling of guilt and then it won't make you anxious by draining your energy in denying that emotion. Once you have accepted it, it is easy to move on. Always remember, it is easiest to forgive ourselves so look within. If it is your fault, accept it. It brings a lot of peace.

Once I kept some jewellery I owned, a little carelessly. I left it on my bed in a bag and went to the other room forgetting all about it and my house help saw the bag and found an opportunity to sneak it out of the house without my knowledge. She stopped coming from the next day and since the bag was out of my sight, I didn't really realise that it was missing until one fine morning when I needed to wear something for a party. I looked for it everywhere and it dawned on me that it was missing. After a lot of brain racking, I remembered that I might have left it on the bed and that was when she stole it and never came back to work after that. Around three months had passed and I had no clue how to trace it back. We decided to report it to the police. Before we could go out to the police station to report it, I asked myself whether I was sure that the house help had taken it. I couldn't be sure because I had not seen her take it. I decided to call her up and ask her. She didn't pick up her phone and when we tried to trace her residence through her identity card, we realised that the address didn't exist. I immediately knew that she was the one. I wanted to find her and shake her up and ask her why she did that to me even after I had been so nice and caring as a boss. Well, for a few days, I was really very morose and full of negativity as I was continuously blaming her for the loss. I had realised that even if I file a complaint it was impossible to find my jewellery back and the fact that there were souvenirs from my grandmother, my mother, my Guru and my husband that had been my prized possessions made me feel dejected and sorrowful for days.

One fine day, while I was in solitude, I realised the fact that I had been careless and had left a bag full of jewellery and some cash on the bed in front of a person who was actually leading a deprived life. I felt bad for the house-help to be put into that state of dilemma where she had to choose between loyalty and a comfortable life. She had a five-year-old son and had dreams of getting a sound education for him and to be able to buy good clothes, good food for her only son. Putting her into that situation was a horrendous crime on my part. I realised that it was actually my fault because of which I had to go through such a tough time of losing my prized possessions and also that she had to go through this dilemma of being honest or choosing the easy way out. When we see the larger picture, the fault was completely mine. I was the

Satan who had made her choose the path of sin.

The moment this realisation dawned on me, I was more relaxed and it was very easy for me to forgive her. The fault was mine. I didn't forgive myself instantly but eventually I did come to terms with the fact that what had gone was gone forever. It was my fault and I should just learn to move on because there was no other way. This realisation saved me from such a lot pain of and anguish that I had been going through that my faith in the fact that 'honesty is the best policy' was restored.

There are situations where telling the truth can really create a problem and to tackle such situations, we end up making excuses. My suggestion is that when we are in such situations where we cannot accept the truth, we must remain silent. Yes, silence is golden because it can really save you from a lot of embarrassment.

Once Buddha was standing on a street doing something. Suddenly a little lamb came running and turned towards the left on the forked road ahead. A few seconds later a butcher with a knife in his hand came running from the same direction. On reaching the fork he got confused. He saw Buddha standing there and asked him, "Did you see a lamb come this way?"

Buddha remained silent. The butcher asked him again, "Tell me, did the lamb go this way?"

He didn't reply. When he asked again, "Did the lamb go left or right?"

Buddha just smiled. The butcher got really frustrated and moved ahead taking one of the roads ahead. Now some of you will say that this doesn't work all the time. I agree. There are times when you can't remain silent because the person asking you could be an authority and in control of your happiness. In such a situation, just tell the truth.

Now let's see the same situation from another perspective. If the person asking Buddha about the lamb had compelled him (though it is a bit unrealistic to believe but we can just assume) in some way or the other, he would have told him that the lamb had passed that way. When he would have asked him whether he took the left or the right, he would have told him that he took the left road. Now that's the maximum he could have done for the lamb, because if you see the larger picture, had he not been there and not seen the scene, he wasn't answerable and the butcher would have gone whichever way he wanted. Since he was there, the only thing that he could do was to delay the butcher from reaching the lamb. Who knows, if it wasn't destined the lamb would have already been saved without anybody's interference.

Whenever you are in a situation of dilemma, choose the truth. It is always going to help you and I can vouch for this in all circumstances.

When we are truthful and honest, we don't have to justify anything. In situations like when we are late for an appointment and we tell the real reasons, it turns out either more hilarious or more empathetic rather than the cliched answers of traffic being high and other such answers.

I remember that I had reached late for a job interview and the reason was that I had overslept. Well, I didn't start with the excuse and didn't get really defensive even though I was ready with my answer honestly. So, I met them confidently and after the entire session they asked me why I was late and I told them that I had overslept and apologised for it. They were amused and we had a great laugh. I realised that the reason wasn't actually important once they had made up their mind. If they had asked me right in the beginning I would have told them the same reason and if they would have got furious I would have been saved the entire process of going through the grilling session and if they would have decided to go ahead with it I would make sure that I impress them enough to not be able to get swayed with that slip.

There is one way to find out if a man is honest – ask him. If he says 'yes', you know he is crooked. Groucho Marx

Well, that doesn't mean one must be late for appointments and expect everyone to understand. But they must definitely understand that you are going to be honest and forthright even when you start working for them as you don't nccd any unhappiness or bad blood in your associations. Miscommunication is also a form of dishonesty so one must stay away from it as much as possible. If through your actions or body language you communicate to people to treat you in a certain way and then you receive that negative treatment you will not like it. So be very honest in your body language and learn to keep it in sync with your words.

When you're dishonest with yourself, you're disconnected from reality. You're going to make poor decisions. You're going to drop out of the moment and you're going to be less happy and you're going to be wrong. -Naval Ravikant

Honesty is the highest form of respect. Before we give this respect to the others, we must give it to ourselves. Being honest to ourselves is what we must start with while trying to master this habit.

To be able to master this habit we need to bring into our routine at least one of the following activities.

1. Meditation- When we are

meditating, we breathe in and breathe out focussing completely on the breath. We feel the air entering our lungs and then the expulsion of the air out of our body through the nostrils. When we focus on our breath and do it regularly, we slowly learn the technique of concentrating only on that present moment and forget all about our past worries or future tensions. That moment of realisation gives us the courage to be ourselves in the present moment.

"Praying is talking to the Universe. Meditation is listening to it." – Paulo Coelho

After this activity we become more aware of the fragility and mortality of our beings. We become humble and sombre and slowly and steadily we become aware of our true self and true acceptance starts seeping into our whole being.

Initially it may seem silly to sit and do nothing but breathe and it may sound boring too but the importance of this simple yet powerful activity has been reiterated by several great personalities.

"Half an hour's meditation each day is essential, except when you are busy. Then a full hour is needed."
– Saint Francis de Sales

Honesty is an awareness that doesn't let any promiscuity touch you and malign you, leaving you in a balanced state of mind which is free from any kind of expectations.

"At the end of the day, I can end up just totally wacky, because I've made mountains out of molehills. With meditation, I can keep them as molehills." – Ringo Starr

2. Writing a journal- Every day

after the hectic hours of the entire day are done, we must sit down and write what the day was like. This helps us analyse the importance of each day, each moment and at times how grateful we are to be full of life and full of these small moments that make our days richer and liveable. Sometimes we also have sad days when we want to forget and erase what happened rather than note it down. Write on those days too. Believe me, it is the best catharsis ever because your diary, your journal is your best friend. You can bare your soul in front of it without fearing judgement.

"This is how you do it: you sit down at the keyboard and you put one word after another until its done. It's that easy, and that hard." - Neil Gaiman

Well, it does seem to be a difficult task to be expressive in writing especially if you aren't the expressive types. But the whole point is that we need to express and it is up to you how and which medium you choose to express yourself. Some really great books were written just by printing journal pages of a great mind. So, you never know, maybe a great story is waiting to be written down in the form of a book through your journal!

"There is nothing to writing. All you do is sit down at a typewriter and bleed." - Ernest Hemingway

Believe Hemingway when he said that. So, grab a diary and start writing your woes away. Be your happy self before you hit the pillow.

3. Meeting yourself in the

mirror- I know people who are great talkers and to the extent that they find their own company the most entertaining. Some of the happiest people are people who talk to themselves and consult themselves for every decision they make.

As Sapadin puts it, "Saying [your goals] out loud focuses your attention, reinforces the message, controls your runaway emotions and screens out distractions."

Gigi Engle reiterates- Talking to yourself means that you are self-reliant. Like Albert Einstein, who "was highly gifted and acquired early in his life the ability to exploit his talents," people who talk to themselves are highly proficient and count on only themselves to figure out what they need.

We "crazies" are the most efficient and intelligent of the bunch. We take the time to listen to our inner voices, out loud and proud!

(Quoted from Elite Daily by Gigi Engle)

There's no specific time to talk to yourself as you can constantly be in touch with yourself. You can consult, discuss, tell, argue, scold or praise yourself whenever you want as you do not need to wait for an appointment or permission to enjoy your own company.

4. Going for a walk- When I say, going for a walk, I don't mean going for a walk with music in your ears or going for a walk with a friend. When you go out in the natural

surroundings for a walk, you meet yourself on the way. You get time alone with yourself, the best company you can ever get. This person you meet knows you thoroughly. This person loves you unconditionally and this person has the most brutal honesty when it comes to criticising you or telling you your strengths and weaknesses. Meet this person every day. Go for a walk every day in a natural surrounding where you don't meet too many people who know you. The trick is to change your route often so that you don't become familiar with people around you as it makes you obliged to acknowledge their presence. The motive, you must remember, is to meet yourself not the others. So, walk and talk and be

with yourself for at least half an hour
every day.

Habit three- Self love

Follow Mahi. Author for more quotes on yourquote.in

Habit three- Self love

"If you could only sense how important you are to the lives of those you meet; how important you can be to people you may never even dream of. There is something of yourself that you leave at every meeting with another person." Fred Rogers (Mr. Rogers)

Believe the words of Fred Rogers like they are the words of the almighty. Yes, when we were created, we were born with an inherent liking for ourselves. We don't have to develop affection for ourselves and that's the purest form of love. Over the years because we are criticised by the others around us because we see people finding things/aspects to dislike about us we start believing their outlook and forget our own.

To get ourselves to love our own being we need to believe that we aren't born to judge everything around us, including ourselves. That's step one. The moment we start realising that there's very little in this world that we can influence we stop becoming harsh in our judgements.

People who are the most cynical are the hardest on themselves. We see around us so much negativity that after a point of time we start internalising it. Take a deep breath, you aren't alone. There are many, sailing on the same boat.

Empathy is the key to deal with developing this habit. Before we discuss this any further, let me tell you that a person who doesn't love himself or herself can never empathise truly. So, first let us analyse what is empathy.

According to the Merriam Webster, empathy is defined as follows:

: the action of understanding, being aware of, being sensitive to, and vicariously experiencing the feelings, thoughts, and experience of another of either the past or present without having the feelings, thoughts, and experience fully communicated in an objectively explicit manner.

Let us break that up for an easier understanding. The action of understanding means trying to understand how the other person is feeling. 'of being sensitive to' means to feel with your senses open. The five senses we have must be involved in understanding how the other person is feeling. 'vicariously experiencing' means to understand through your imagination how another must be feeling or what he or she must be going through. While we are expected to understand all this and more, we must remember that all this has to be felt and experienced not expressed.

It is important to understand that why it is not to be expressed in words because generally, when people need empathy, they are in a vulnerable situation and any wrong word can create a long term hurt or make them feel that your concern is fake.

The same concept of empathy applies to your own self. Do not say that you love yourself or really respect yourself and then go ahead and demean yourself or fail in your own eyes. Respect 'self-dignity' not just when you are alone but also when you are in a crowd.

So many times, you see people around you who compromise with their dignity, to be successful in the eyes of others. They need a promotion so they'll lick the boots of their bosses and climb the ladder of success. This kind of success never brings happiness because you never gain the respect you have lost in your own eyes. A person who doesn't value himself can never be happy. There are other ways of gaining a promotion- work hard!

In the long run what matters is your mental health, your own image in the most important person's eyes- YOUSELF!

To develop this strong habit, one must ask themselves how they would feel about another person in the same position. The most important aspect of empathy isn't only when we need to be compassionate to others but also when we need to analyse our own actions.

To develop self-love, we must:

ı   Have a positive body image which is possible through a regular routine to keep one fit and healthy. Being too fat or too thin is not what body image is about. We must learn to be comfortable with what we look like. We must never compare ourselves with anyone or ridicule ourselves for not having a slimmer figure, a better nose, a perfect set of teeth or evenlong wavy hair. Whatever we have we must be accepting of it and if there's scope of improvement we must work towards it. If you look nice wearing makeup do wear it often so that you look good to yourself.

Talk to yourself politely-So many times, you must have heard people say things like, "Why am I so stupid?" or "Couldn't expect better from a dumbass like me!" Well, never ridicule yourself even in isolation. The moment you catch yourself being impolite to your own self- stop!

Sometimes people say in jest, "I am such a bitch!" just to validate that they are doing something wrong but they approve of it. Well, if you approve of it, then it is your choice and you do not need to justify it. Don't call yourself names for it. If you feel the need to do so, don't do that thing. If you still need to do it, do not call yourself names! Instead you can say, "I know this is against my nature but the other person deserves it."

꘎ Look for ways to appreciate yourself- When after a hard day you go to bed, list out at least one or two things that you like about yourself. Think about it deeply and appreciate the fact that not everyone has the same quality that you have. Appreciate that in this hard world it isn't easy to continue being the good self that you are. Appreciate your talents and thank yourself for being who you are. Some people can say that you can't think of anything good that you can give yourself credit for. Well, think hard and you will find it. We tend to take ourselves for granted and that is one big reason why people around us take us for granted. The day you learn to value yourself you will see how the perspectives of people around you change too.

The only fear is that one must remember the fine line between genuine self-love and false ego. Be honest to yourself and don't just sing, "I'm the best, I'm the best!" live up to it. Don't disappoint yourself.

"When you are joyful, when you say yes to life and have fun and project positivity all around you, you become a sun in the centre of every constellation, and people want to be near you."— Shannon L. Alder

Habit four- Attitude

Follow Mahi. Author for more quotes on yourquote.in

Habit four- Attitude

There can be thousands of reasons to be unhappy but one reason to be happy, choose it. After all, no one is going to live your life for you so why shouldn't you make it worthwhile for yourself?

"Life is a bowl of cherries. Some cherries are rotten while others are good; it's your job to throw out the rotten ones and forget about them while you enjoy eating the ones that are good! There are two kinds of people: those who choose to throw out the good cherries and wallow in all the rotten ones, and those who choose to throw out all the rotten ones and savour all the good ones."
— C. Joy Bell C.

Having a positive attitude is imperative to be a happy person. I have a friend who has seen the most difficult of phases in life but whenever you meet her, she is so full of positivity that wherever she goes she is accepted with open arms. What she teaches me is that when a person like her who has seen all kinds of sufferings in life and is still fighting with health issues, monetary issues and family issues; can be so full of vitality and positivity what reasons do I have to sit down and feel dejected in life. Look around and you will find that the person who is the most positive and full of compassion has been through the most harrowing circumstances in life and they still choose to be positive and happy. This attitude towards life is what keeps them going strong.

To maintain your sanity and your positivity-

1. Try to have at least one such

person who inspires you to look towards life differently. When you look around and meet people, observe them and see what makes them tick. When you see that there are people who are harrowed and low, analyse how there are so many things they should be happy about. Tell them and generate that confidence in them to like themselves and be kind towards themselves. Doing this will help you become a more positive person too. So basically, get motivated from people around you and pass on that motivation to whoever needs it. This will start the cycle of positivity which will radiate your own life forever.

2. Meditate- Once again,

meditation or spending silent time with yourself will remind you of your self-worth which will motivate you to be your best self. When you go through dark phases of life- losing a spouse, losing a job, losing a loved one to death, losing a great friend; it isn't easy to continue being positive and enthusiastic. In fact, it is unnatural to deny yourself the time to heal from these situations but during the time that you are healing do continue to meditate and remind yourself that you are more than these incidents.

3. Time is the best healer and

change is the only constant. There have been times when I felt that my life can never recover from the damage that I was going through but years later when I look back at these events, I realise that they were important events too because they have made me what I am today. Keep that faith and deal with life as a learning experience. Heal from the wounds of life and keep each scar as a medal for your achievements.

I read somewhere that your positive attitude may not solve all your problems but it will definitely help you annoy your enemies and make it worth your while. So, smile the clouds away and remember that, that is the only way to keep the darkness out of your life!

4. Music therapy- heals your bad mood and makes you positive again. Music has a lot of potential to

change your day from morose to rocking. So, play on- listen, sing, dance to your favourite tune but do indulge yourself. Reading poetry helps too. The world could be a brutal place at times and we need to escape into the world of poetry to enliven our spirits. Once we have rejuvenated our senses, we must expose ourselves back to this world with the wisdom that all of life is transient and we cannot afford to lose the time that is constantly ticking away.

Habit five- Dreams and Goals

Dare to dive
Rev up your skills
Expect to excel
Aspire to win
Motivate yourself and
Success will kiss your feet!

– Mahi_Author

Follow Mahi. Author for more quotes on yourquote.in

Habit five- Dreams and Goals

You see things and you say, 'Why?'. But I dream things and I say, 'Why not?'. - George Bernard Shaw

The biggest motivation in life is when we have goals and aspirations to achieve. If life is mundane and lacks dreams and aspirations, we lose the spark that is essential for a fulfilling life.

There's a difference between wishful thinking and aspiring towards a goal. So wishful thinking keeps you busy in happy thoughts but it isn't long-lasting as sooner or later you realise that this would never be accomplished because all goals to be accomplished require proper planning and execution of it. An aspiration becomes a concrete reality only when it is backed by hard work, strategic planning to achieve the desired goals and objectives.

Let's plan according to the following acrostic:

D Dare to dream

R Reach out to achieve them

E Encourage yourself everyday

A Aim with a plan in mind

M Maintain consistency of effort

S Speak less, work more.

1. Now let's analyse it step by step. When we dare to dream, we challenge ourselves to go beyond our ordinary lives and wish for ourselves what we generally don't think can be possible.

2. When we have dreamt to be at a particular position in life, we start to want it passionately. To be able to achieve our dreams and goals we are expected to strategize and plan to achieve them. Basically, having a dream keeps us busy so that we can

have something positive to think about. Something that deviates your mind from the present drudgery of life. If there's some negativity you get motivated by thinking that your future isn't going to be the same. When you get that push, you plan with your heart and soul to change the situation which saddens you or makes you dull.

"If you want to be happy, set a goal that commands your thoughts, liberates your energy and inspires your hopes." —*Andrew Carnegie*

3. Encourage yourself everyday

to achieve your goals and keep your focus on the sunny dreams than on the present circumstances if they aren't as you desire. When we say that one must encourage themselves, we must beware of the fact that it doesn't trap you and make you overambitious. Encourage yourself honestly. If you know in your heart that the dream you have conceived is not going to be accomplished without hurting people, weigh the pros and cons. No one except you, is a better judge of analysing whether the dream you have is worth being accomplished. Once you have ascertained that your dream is the most desirable and satisfying thing you want, preparations should begin towards achieving it. The busier you are the better you will feel towards your own self.

Remember nothing succeeds better than hard work!

'We grow great by dreams. All big men are dreamers. They see things in the soft haze of a spring day or in the red fire of a long winter's evening. Some of us let these great dreams die, but others nourish and protect them; nurse them through bad days till they bring them to the sunshine and light which comes always to those who sincerely hope that their dreams will come true' - Woodrow Wilson

4. Aim with a plan in mind-
A goal without a plan is just a wish."
~ Antoine de Saint-Exupéry. Therefore, it is indispensable in the scheme of things. When working towards a happy life we must plan how we will bring it about in our lives. Planning keeps you positively engaged. It keeps you motivated towards a brighter future.

Like I have said in one of my own poems- Destination is not the only goal, the journey carries joys manifold.

The journey comprises of planning, choosing the course of action, the instruments required to achieve what we aspire.

"For tomorrow belongs to those who prepare for it today!' African Proverb.

5. Maintain consistency of effort-

The famous story of the two frogs who fell in the bucket of milk is the best analogy to abide by.

So, there were two frogs who fell in a bucket of milk. The first frog thought that this was the end of his life and because of his negative attitude, it slowly died. The other frog wasn't ready to accept this fate so he continued to jump up trying to get out of the bucket. There was constant movement and that created the milk to curdle and then form butter. After hours of struggling, a thick layer of butter was formed which helped the frog get a base on which he climbed and then jumped out of the bucket. Therefore, we can see how constant striving helped the frog come out of a critical situation which could have resulted in its death.

Sharpening the saw is very important before you cut down the tree. If you use a blunt saw to cut the tree down you will not just take more time but also have more chances of failure. What I am suggesting here is that one must strive constantly so that the saw is always sharp and ready for use.

Like our elders have said that 'practice makes one perfect' we must continuously practice whatever is imperative to gain our goals. It helps us in two ways- one that we become perfect in our pursuit and the other that we are positively engaged which gives us no time to be sad or unhappy or lonely.

Conversations and open communication have been stressed as important habits for achieving success but then the next point

6. Speak less, work more- might seem a bit of a tricky point. Do not panic because this doesn't mean you must drown into your work and not socialise. Socializing is very important for a sane existence. What I mean here is that if we proclaim

our ideas and dreams lightly and in front of everyone, all the time they lose the importance that we must attach to them. We tend to take our dreams a bit for granted if we talk too much about it. What we need to do instead is, to talk to ourselves often and reiterate what we have decided for ourselves.

When we talk to the others about our dreams and they take it lightly or make fun of it or give it no importance we feel disheartened and thus lose motivation to accomplish it. It might result in an increased amount of vengeance too which could spurt us forward but what we are looking for is not a spurt but a positive aura around us.

When I say don't speak, it doesn't mean we need to necessarily work secretly towards the goal we have. We must consult and confide in people we trust and love. Just talking about it all the time takes away a lot of our energy and we feel satisfied for the time being and that spurt or fire to achieve it becomes a bit dowsed for some time. We need to keep the fire burning and therefore continue to strive for achieving your dreams instead of speaking about it and building other peoples' expectations from you. Whatever you want to do, do it for yourself. Remember the rule of self-love!

Habit six- Conversation

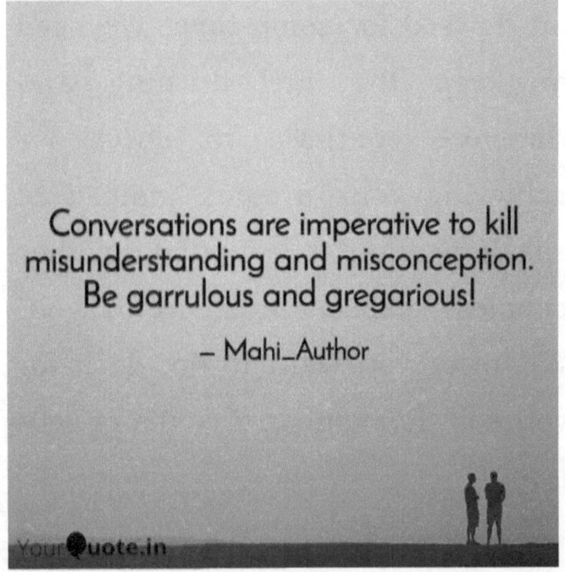

Follow Mahi. Author for more quotes on yourquote.in

Habit six- Conversation

The great gift of conversation lies less in displaying it ourselves than in drawing it out of others. He who leaves your company pleased with himself and his own cleverness is perfectly well pleased with you.

Jean de La Bruyère

Well, conversations as said by Jean de La Bruyère is more about drawing out of others than speaking too much to bore the others. The most important thing about conversations is that it is two sided.

I have met a lot of people who think they are great conversationalists but it turned out that they were huge bores and people around them did not like them much because they used to talk too much about themselves and usually the conversation consisted of them talking the most. So imperative life lesson: conversations are supposed to be two sided.

Listening with empathy is an important aspect of conversations. Now, you must be thinking that how can a person who is immersed in sadness be an open listener? Well, that's where empathy creeps in. when you are sad and in no mood to entertain anyone you can be a good listener as it not just shifts your focus from your own problem but also gives you something else to think about. When we understand the other person's problem, we start evaluating it with our own and that sometimes exposes the triviality of our own sorrows or problems.

We also get another person to share our problems with and it surely helps as two minds are better than one and the solution can be easily achieved.

So many times, we are sad, depressed or misunderstood by another person. Instead of sulking, be strong enough to take the first step, and sort things out. This may not be easy but it definitely lifts the burden off your shoulders and you can sleep peacefully because you have taken the first step. You have tried to solve the issue. There's no guilt and that gives you the freedom to smile and rejoice unlike the other person who still feels burdened and depressed because s/he couldn't use the opportunity to make it up with you. Most of the times though, it works out as no one wants to lose friends or well wishers over small misunderstandings.

Taking the first step doesn't mean to apologize even when you aren't wrong. It means to clarify where you are coming from, what you mean and why you said a particular thing. It could also mean that you want to enquire what the other person meant and where s/he is coming from. Maybe you did not completely understand what s/he meant and took it to your heart whereas the other person was in a different zone altogether. Clarifying things out will help in all such cases.

Sometimes we do not have people whom we can confide in. We do something we feel is bad or something has happened and we have nobody to converse with or share our sorrows with. In such a case like we have discussed earlier, it is very important to vent out any negative emotion that may be building up inside of you. It could be anger, hatred, sorrow, tension, weakness, jealousy, guilt; but we need to get rid of it. The question is How?

Well, talk to yourself. Go to an empty room, or to a beautiful place near a lake, mountain, river, waterfall, and if nothing is possible, go to your own washroom and talk to yourself loudly. Talk as if you are talking to someone else who has no clue of what happened. Have a full-fledged conversation and you will see that your emotions that were gnawing at your conscience and peace of mind will vent out. Be very straightforward. Talk loudly as you would talk to another person. No inhibitions. Just talk. And remember, it isn't insane to talk to yourself. Most of the wise people find their own company the most interesting and the most motivating. They all talk to themselves. Why do you think we have soliloquys, and monologues in Literature? It is the most effective way to connect to your inner self. The characters have conversations with themselves because that's a natural way to express and it is natural to find your company more interesting than any one else's.

The important points to remember while conversing:

1. Listen more than speaking

2. Speak clearly and empathically.
3. Think before you speak.
4. Listening is an important part of conversing.
5. Listen not to answer, but to understand.
6. It is important to talk your heart out rather than regret later.
7. If you can converse with someone for hours without feeling uncomfortable, marry him/her. S/he's rare!

Conversations make bonds stronger and avoid misunderstandings and misrepresentations as when you can get it from the horse's mouth, why not?

Habit seven- Gratitude

Follow Mahi.Author on yourquote.in for more quotes

Habit seven- Gratitude

"Gratitude is not only the greatest of virtues but the parent of all others."
– Marcus Tullius Cicero

The more gratitude we have the better we feel about ourselves. It is a great anti-depressant though it isn't very easy to master.

When we are deeply hurt or sad, we tend to sympathize with ourselves and we pity ourselves for being in a sorry state. Sometimes we even judge ourselves harshly and get angry for something that isn't even in our control. We have to stop and analyze that whether we really need to be that negative about that situation.

Thinking about what worse could have happened and analyzing what we do have that can make us happy, will solve our misery and bring back joy.

When we get up in the morning and sit up straight on our beds thinking about how we are going to start the day, we must add a list of five things at least for which we should be grateful in life. The first thing could always be that you have survived another day and have a whole new day in front of you. So many people pass away in their sleep every day. Not everyone makes it to a new day every day, so be thankful that you are alive and have a bright day ahead of you which you can make the most of.

Be thankful if you have a job, a bank account, a family, a house, a healthy body, a friend, education, your parents, your children, your spouse, your boyfriend, your mentor and above everything a life that you can make the most of.

'Nick Vujicic' the greatest motivational speaker I have ever come across, who walks the talk he gives, is the most inspiring person you can ever meet. Listen to his talks, watch his videos and for the ones who are not aware, you will be surprised to see that he has neither legs nor hands but he is the most self sufficient and independent person, oozing life from every iota of his being. If he can be grateful, everyone ought to be. If he could make it in life and be such a huge inspiration for everyone, anyone who complains has no reason what soever. 'It only takes a spark, to get a fire going!' Get that spark.

"Let us rise up and be thankful, for if we didn't learn a lot today, at least we learned a little, and if we didn't learn a little, at least we didn't get sick, and if we got sick, at least we didn't die; so, let us all be thankful."
– Buddha

Extra Dose-Stay away from denial

Follow Mahi. Author for more quotes on yourquote.in

The biggest reason for unhappiness is the denial of emotions.

Sometimes we are elated and joyful but we feel guilty of being that happy. Yes, you heard me right. There are times when we feel guilty for being happy. Just analyze and if the cause for your guilt is that you've hurt someone- rectify it.

To be completely and blissfully happy you need to be the most honest with yourself. Be in constant touch with your emotions, your conscience and keep track of your thoughts. If you see yourself losing your peace of mind, remember that it is in your control. Before it escalates out of proportion, control it by solving the issue in its roots.

If you are angry or jealous, don't deny yourself the luxury of expressing it. Accept the feeling, vent it out through the various methods learnt above and move on. If you are angry with another person, just sit down, analyze and try to scold that person or forgive that person. Just communicate and if the person is unavailable or you know that you can't really vent it out on him or her (could be your boss

) just imagine that the person is there and scold to your heart's content.

Then, move on.

Empathizing helps too. Sometimes, you don't know where a person is coming from, what pressures, grievances and personal problems the person who has angered you is carrying. Try to give that benefit of doubt once, twice, thrice. If it's a pattern and a regular thing just ignore him/her as a blabbering idiot. Smile. Move on. Know that the problem lies with the other person, not you!

Be honest with yourself.

Talk to yourself.

Be thankful for what you have.

Enjoy your solitude.

Meditate.

Listen to music / Play music.

Dance.

Read.

Write/Talk/Express

Build your positive aura

SMILE OFTEN!!

AUTHOR INTRODUCTION

Mahi describes herself as a *crazy* English teacher who is loved by her students. She is blessed to have wonderful and happy children around her. She is passionate and innovative in her classroom and her children feel safe, comfortable and connected. She writes to be able to express herself creatively. Her thoughts and ideas are liberal and modern and the setting of her stories are contemporary; sometimes rural sometimes urban.

This is her third book and her first non-fiction venture. She has already published two anthologies named **Memoirs- a collection of short stories** and **Blue God and other stories** which have been appreciated widely. She is looking forward to an even better reception of her third book as she has already created a niche and is growing with each book. She has had many years of teaching experience in India and abroad. She loves to travel and enjoys different cultures. Her hobbies are reading, listening to music; mostly Ghazals, old Hindi songs and English country music. She enjoys the natural flora and fauna of the world. Concrete jungles and trendy fashions are not her cup of tea as she believes in simple living and a humble existence.

She has a son who shares a beautiful bond of friendship with his mom and a husband who is a perfect soulmate because...you know, opposites attract!!

Follow the Author@

**https://www.facebook.com/mahimishra 007/
as Creative juices**

www.mahimamishra.wordpress.com

Mahi.author on Instagram

**Or write to her
mahima.tsms@gmail.com**